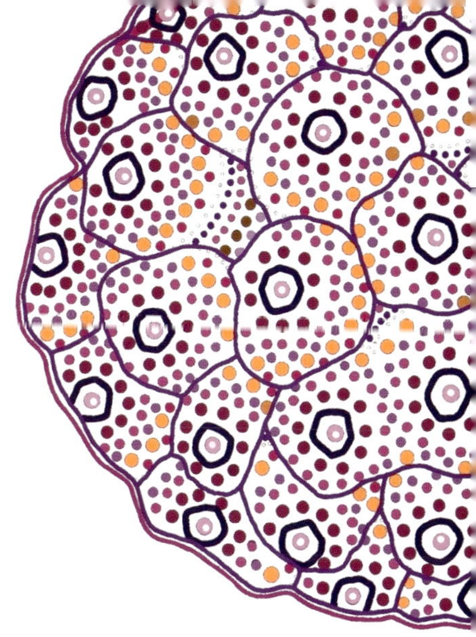

DEADLY SCIENCE

The solar system

Contents:

ADJUNCT ASSOCIATE PROFESSOR COREY TUTT OAM

DEADLY SCIENCE

DeadlyScience aims to provide Science, Technology, Engineering and Mathematics (STEM) resources to remote schools around Australia. So far, DeadlyScience has shipped more than shipped more than 33,000 STEM books and resources to more than 800 schools across the country.

The organisation began when proud Kamilaroi man Corey Tutt found out that some schools in Australia were completely under-resourced and that Aboriginal and Torres Strait Islander children were discouraged from pursuing STEM because of this. DeadlyScience knows from personal experience that books and resources change lives and believes these kids deserve nothing but the best. Aboriginal and Torres Strait Islander peoples in Australia were the First Scientists of this land, and DeadlyScience is committed to preserving that history.

Our universe

We may think the Earth is enormous, but it is just one of eight planets in our solar system. Our solar system is probably one of billions of such systems in our galaxy (the Milky Way), and the Milky Way is just one of billions of galaxies in the universe. The universe is made up of everything that exists in space, and it stretches for billions of kilometres. It's tricky to understand just how huge it is, but even if you were travelling at the speed of light, it would take you more than 13.8 billion years to cross the known universe. Some scientists believe that our universe might even be just one of several universes!

Our solar system

The Sun is at the centre of the solar system. Orbiting the Sun are eight planets, including Earth, and also several dwarf planets, such as Pluto.

What a view ...

When astronauts on *Apollo 8* flew to the Moon in 1968, they observed the cloudy blue Earth rising into view. In comparison, the Moon they were orbiting was just a lifeless grey globe. One astronaut, Jim Lovell, said of space, 'The vast loneliness is awe-inspiring.'

Earth

Our planet gets its heat and light from a star – the Sun. No other planets with life have yet been found, although several planets that may be able to support life have been found.

Well, hello!

Our nearest neighbour is the Moon. Others are the planets, dwarf planets, and the Sun, which make up our solar system. Travelling at the speed of light, it would take one second to travel to the Moon, eight minutes to the Sun, and four hours to Neptune.

We have lift off!

First Nations Australians are one step closer to going into space, with students Giovanni D'Urso and Tui Nolan being selected to do work experience with the Jet Propulsion Lab at NASA. Wiradjuri astrophysicist Kirsten Banks and Kamilaroi astronomer and astrophysicist Karlie Noon are also studying our vast universe.

Far, far away

The light from the most distant galaxies we can see departed those distant objects more than 13 billion years ago.

Our neighbours

A galaxy is a group of stars and planets held together by gravity. Galaxies are different shapes and sizes, but they tend to group in clusters. The closest galaxies to ours form a cluster known as the Local Group. The Andromeda galaxy is the closest large galaxy to ours.

Reach for the stars

Travelling at the speed of light, it would take about 200,000 years to cross our galaxy, the Milky Way. The Milky Way is made up of approximately 100 billion stars, and our Sun is just one of them!

DID YOU KNOW?

On clear nights from March to August, you may see the dark 'Emu in the Sky' from First Nations astronomy. It's created by the dark areas of the sky between the stars.

The Big Bang

Our universe is larger than we can imagine. But many billions of years ago, it was all packed into a space smaller than a microscopic dot. Then, about 13.7 billion years ago, a dramatic expansion began in a process scientists refer to as the Big Bang. This was the start of the universe as we know it, and it is still expanding. The initial flash of energy was extremely hot – billions of times hotter than the surface of our Sun. Since then, the universe has been cooling.

The history of time

In a super-hot, dense flash of energy, the universe blew up in size. In this brief moment, space and time began.

1. In the first three minutes, the universe that we know started as atomic particles.
2. Cooling caused clouds of gas to form.
3. Lumps of gas became the first stars.
4. Gas clouds collided to form galaxies.
5. Spinning discs of gas and dust formed stars and planets.

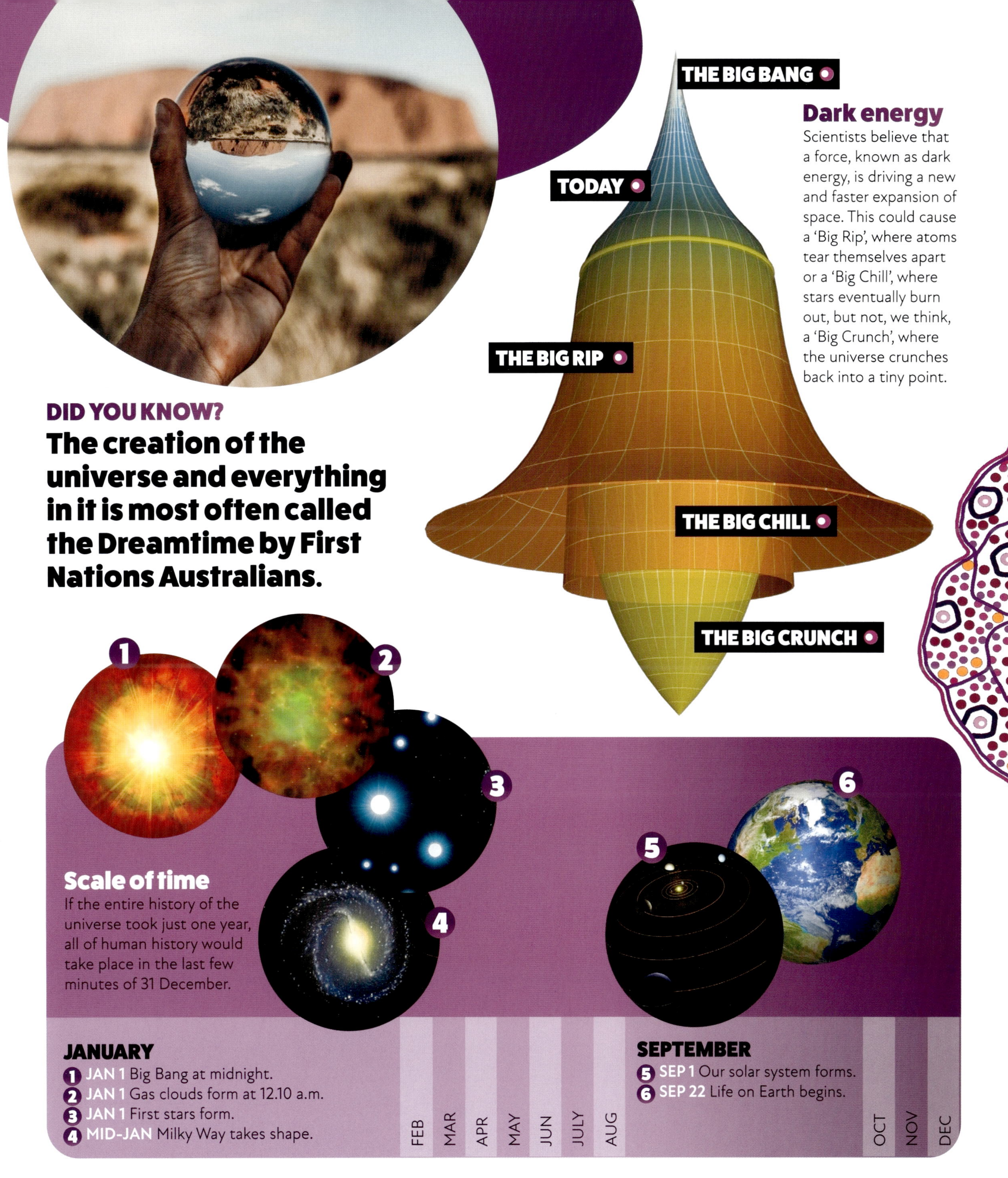

Dark energy

Scientists believe that a force, known as dark energy, is driving a new and faster expansion of space. This could cause a 'Big Rip', where atoms tear themselves apart or a 'Big Chill', where stars eventually burn out, but not, we think, a 'Big Crunch', where the universe crunches back into a tiny point.

DID YOU KNOW?

The creation of the universe and everything in it is most often called the Dreamtime by First Nations Australians.

Scale of time

If the entire history of the universe took just one year, all of human history would take place in the last few minutes of 31 December.

JANUARY

1. JAN 1 Big Bang at midnight.
2. JAN 1 Gas clouds form at 12.10 a.m.
3. JAN 1 First stars form.
4. MID-JAN Milky Way takes shape.

SEPTEMBER

5. SEP 1 Our solar system forms.
6. SEP 22 Life on Earth begins.

Our solar system

A solar system refers to a star and all the different bodies that orbit around it. Our solar system includes all the planets, comets and asteroids that move around the Sun. You could think of it as Earth's neighbourhood, with the other planets in our solar system being our neighbours.

Hello, neighbour!

Our solar system can be divided into three main zones. First there is the Sun, around which the planets and other bodies orbit. It provides the heat and light that we need to survive. The Sun is a big ball of gas that burns about 4 million tonnes of gas every second, and it is roughly 100 times the diameter of the Earth. Scientists think that the Sun has been shining for about 5 billion years – and that it's probably got another 5 billion years left in it! Next, there is the inner region, which is home to the terrestrial planets: Mercury, Venus, Earth and Mars. It also contains an asteroid belt between the orbits of Mars and Jupiter, where boulders of rock and iron can be found. The outer region is home to the giant planets: Jupiter, Saturn, Uranus and Neptune. Dwarf planets and comets are found beyond here, out in the Kuiper Belt.

First astronomers

Indigenous Australians are the world's first astronomers. Aboriginal and Torres Strait Islander peoples have many different stories for the same constellations.

BUNDJIL

The distinctive Southern Cross constellation is widely viewed as a significant astronomical symbol by Indigenous groups. For Victoria's Kulin Nation people, based around Melbourne, the Southern Cross represents Bundjil, a sky god in the form of an eagle. The Arrernte people of Central Australia see the Southern Cross as the wedge-tailed eagle Waluwarra. The four bright stars make up his talons, and the dark Coalsack Nebula is his nest.

For the Anindilyakwa of Groote Eylandt, in the Gulf of Carpentaria, the Southern Cross represents two fishermen and their cooking fires.

Coastal SA's Ngarrindjeri people see the Southern Cross as a stingray chased by two sharks – the two pointers adjacent the cross. The shark is a sacred Ngarrindjeri totem.

DID YOU KNOW?

It takes our solar system 230 million years to do just one orbit of our galactic centre.

The right stuff

The terrestrial planets (Mercury, Venus, Earth and Mars) are small, rocky and metallic, with solid surfaces. The gas giant planets (Jupiter, Saturn, Uranus and Neptune) are made up mostly of lightweight gases and liquids, and they do not have surfaces.

What's in a name?

All the planets, except one, are named after Roman gods. The odd one out is Earth.

Stars

Just like our Sun, stars are big balls of gas that give off light and heat. They're mostly made of hydrogen and helium – there's an ongoing process at the centre of the star that burns up the hydrogen and converts it into helium. When they burn up all of the hydrogen, they start burning the helium, beginning the next stage in the life cycle of a star. Stars have different temperatures, and those different temperatures give them their colour. The hottest stars are bluish-white, and they burn their hydrogen quickly. Red stars are the coolest, and they burn their gas more slowly. Yellow stars, like ours, are right in the middle.

BLACK HOLE

DID YOU KNOW?

If you get too close to a black hole, you will be spaghettified – pulled and compressed at the same time!

NEBULA

Nurseries

Stars are formed inside nebulae. Nebulae are clouds filled with dust and gases. Turbulence can cause material in the cloud to collapse together and heat up. When the centre of these swirling clouds finally ignites, stars are born.

Growing pains

Stars that are up to 2 times the size of our Sun are known as low-mass stars and stay in this category for around 10 billion years.

Real giants

When massive stars start burning their helium, they expand and become supergiants. These are the biggest kind of star – they can be up to 800 times the size of our Sun! The biggest supergiant stars are known as hypergiants, and they're extremely rare. There's only a handful in the Milky Way galaxy.

RED SUPERGIANT STAR

CRUX

Gacrux (γ)

μ

δ

Mimosa (β)

ε

Coalsack Nebula

Acrux (α)

θ

ζ

η

SOUTHERN CROSS

Big and small

As giants burn up their helium, they shrink again, becoming a planetary nebula. The outer layers of the stars are swept off, creating gas clouds.

Watch out!

When the supergiant burns the last of the helium, the core of the star explodes! This is called a supernova. The huge explosion creates an enormous burst of light, the temperature hits more than 100 billion degrees Celsius, and the star shrinks.

Aftermath

After all the outer layers are gone, and just the burnt, shrunken cores of the stars remain, they are called white dwarves. They slowly cool down – although this is a very long process that takes billions of years.

Transformation

Smaller supergiants become compact, dense neutron stars. They have extremely intense gravitational and magnetic fields.

Lights out

The biggest stars become black holes, which are dense objects with stronger gravitational forces than anything else nearby.

TASMANIA

DID YOU KNOW?

First Nations Australians were the first astronomers, looking to the stars at least 65,000 years ago!

Pluto and the Dwarf Planets

Once considered the ninth planet, Pluto has since been reclassified as a dwarf planet. The other biggest dwarf planets in our solar system are Eris, Ceres, Haumea and Makemake. Pluto and its largest moon, Charon, are so small that both could fit across the width of the USA with room to spare. Dwarf planets are smooth and round, like planets, but without the gravitational pull necessary to have cleared the area around them.

Pluto

Pluto is 5 billion kilometres from Earth, and it has five moons. One day on Pluto equates to 153 hours. It is covered in icy mountains (some as high as 3000 m) and plains made of frozen nitrogen gas, with the temperatures getting to as low as -220 °C. Some scientists have speculated that the interior of Pluto is far warmer and could even house an underground ocean deep in its interior.

Fly by

This composite of enhanced colour images of Pluto and Charon (upper left) was taken by NASA's *New Horizons* spacecraft as it passed through the Pluto system on 14 July 2015.

VENETIA BURNEY

What's in a name?

Pluto was named for the Roman god of the underworld by an 11-year-old girl named Venetia Burney. Even cooler is that in 2014, a group of ground depressions on the planet were named 'Djanggawul Fossae' after three First Nations ancestor beings who travelled between the island of the dead and Australia.

Objects in orbit

Similar to comets, Pluto, Eris and many other Kuiper Belt objects travel around the Sun in elliptical orbits, taking centuries to make one circuit of the Sun. By comparison, the orbits of the eight major planets are more like circles.

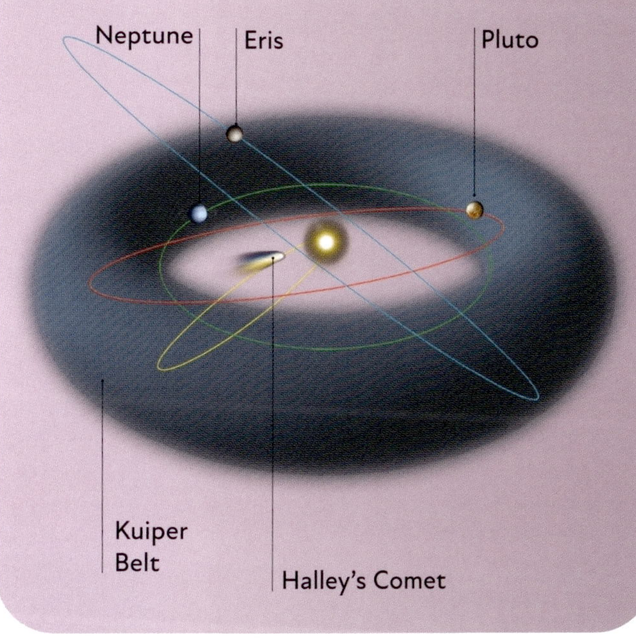

DID YOU KNOW?

NASA's *New Horizons* probe revealed snow-capped chains of mountains on Pluto!

Pluto's five moons

1. Styx (for the river separating the living from the dead) was discovered in 2012 and is 10–24 km across.
2. Nix (for the Greek goddess of darkness, mother of Charon) was discovered in 2005 and is 49.8 km across.
3. Kerberos (named after the three-headed dog from Greek mythology) was discovered in 2011. It is up to 8 km across on its bigger lobe and up to 5 km across on its smaller lobe.
4. Hydra (for the multi-head serpent from Greek and Roman mythology) was discovered in 2005. It is 32–112 km wide and is known as the 'fuzzy dot' by NASA because so little is known about it. This is the best picture of it so far.
5. Charon (for the ferryman who carried souls across the river to the underworld) was discovered in 1978. This moon is approximately 1200 km in diameter.

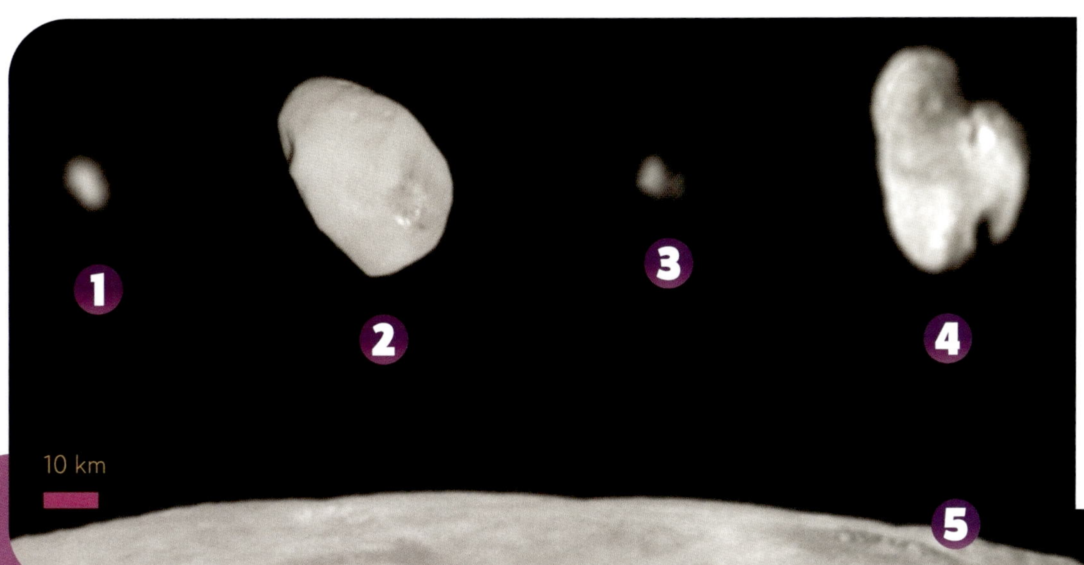

Neptune

An ice giant, Neptune is the last known planet in the solar system and is more than 4.5 billion kilometres from the Sun. Neptune was the first planet that was predicted to exist before it was discovered. Astronomers detected that the orbit of Uranus was being impacted by the gravity of a different body nearby, and their calculations led to Neptune's discovery in 1846.

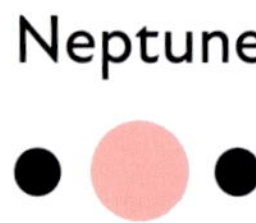

Fountain of Neptune, Bologna, Italy.

Hot, hot, hot!

Neptune is warmer than expected for a planet so far from the Sun, emitting double the energy it receives from the Sun. Astronomers have determined it has an internal heat source, which may be an outcome of ongoing compression of the planetary gases.

What's in a name?

Neptune is named for the Roman god of the sea, and Triton is the name of his son. Triton is the only moon in the solar system that doesn't orbit in the same direction as the rotation of its planet.

And the winner is ...

Even though Uranus has more than twice as many moons as Neptune, Neptune's moons weigh more due to Triton's large size and mass. Triton has a diameter of 2700 km. Triton is also one of the coolest places in our solar system, with a surface temperature of -235 °C. Closer to home, the north pole of our Moon has permanently shadowed craters that have been measured at -273 °C, 100 °C below the temperature that would cause atoms to stop moving.

Fire in the sky

One of Neptune's moons, Triton, is littered with huge geysers that spew liquid nitrogen into the air before it falls over the moon as nitrogen frost. Triton, Io (a moon of Jupiter), Venus and Earth are the only places in our solar system with known volcanic activity.

DID YOU KNOW?

The only spacecraft to have ever orbited Neptune was NASA's *Voyager 2*, which did a fly-by on 25 August 1989.

Uranus

When Uranus was discovered in 1781, it doubled the known size of our solar system. Uranus is a gas giant that's sometimes also known as an ice giant. It's four times the size of Earth, and the temperature at the cloud tops is approximately -216 °C.

FACT

Uranus's equator is severely tilted. Scientists think this could have been caused by a collision with an Earth-sized object in the past.

The big blue

This planet also has rings, although they're narrow and were only discovered in 1977. If you could see them, you would notice that the rings circle around the top and bottom of the planet. That's because Uranus rotates on its side compared to the other planets in our solar system. Uranus has 27 known moons, most of which are composed of water, ice and rocks. Like the other gas planets, the atmosphere of Uranus is mostly made up of hydrogen and helium, but methane gas is also present. It is this gas that lends Uranus its soft blue colour.

DID YOU KNOW?

On Uranus, one day lasts for approximately 17 hours. It takes about 84 Earth years to complete a single orbit of the Sun.

DID YOU KNOW?

Indigenous Australians paid special attention to stars, from the brightest to the faintest – all were given importance.

Well spotted!

When the rings of Uranus were discovered, it wasn't because someone spotted them. Astronomers noticed that as the planet passed in front of a star, the light flickered. They realised that the planet had rings that blocked the light of the star as the planet moved across it. This technique for spotting things – looking for flickers in the light of stars – is the method that astronomers now use to find faraway planets.

False identity

The seventh planet from the Sun, Uranus was originally thought to be either a star or a comet when it was discovered.

What's in a name?

Uranus is named for the Greek god of the sky. Uranus's 27 moons are named after characters written about by authors William Shakespeare and Alexander Pope, such as Oberon, Ariel and Umbriel.

WILLIAM SHAKESPEARE

Epsilon Ring

Some of Uranus's smaller moons circle the planet just outside its bright Epsilon Ring.

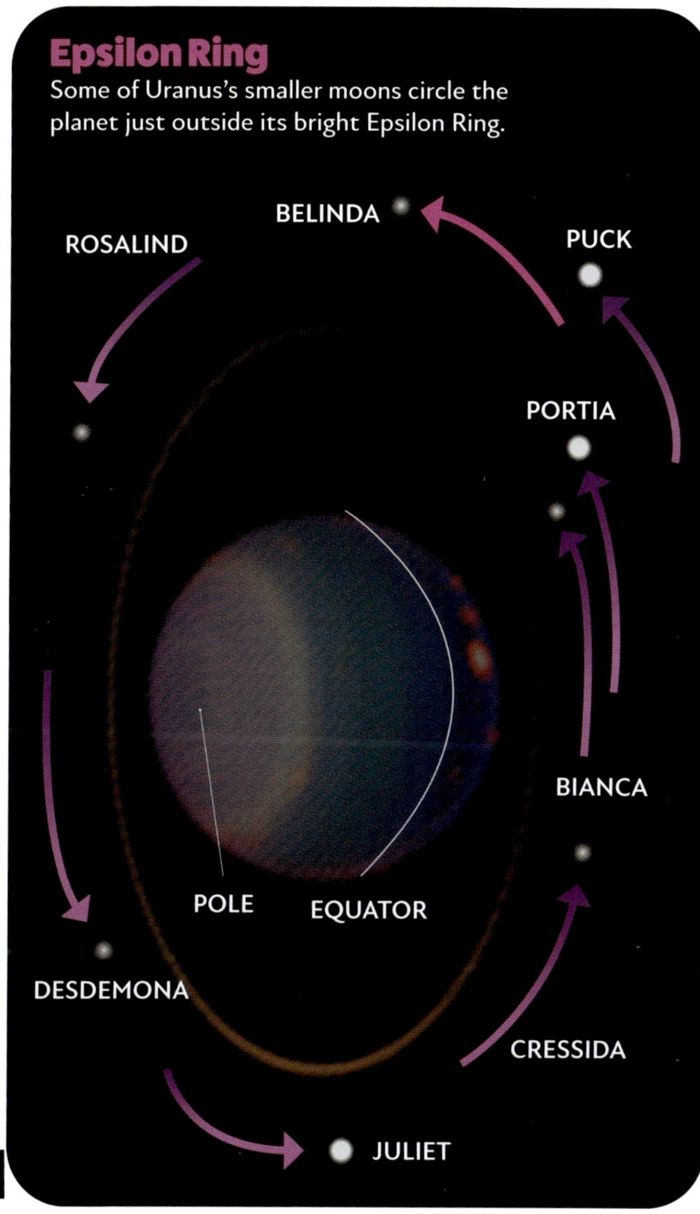

Many moons

Uranus's five major moons vary in size, with each having a radius between 240 km and 800 km.

Saturn

Saturn's rings are its most distinctive feature. They are thought to be made up of fragments from comets, asteroids or shattered moons that have been pulled into orbit. Each ring orbits the planet at a different speed.

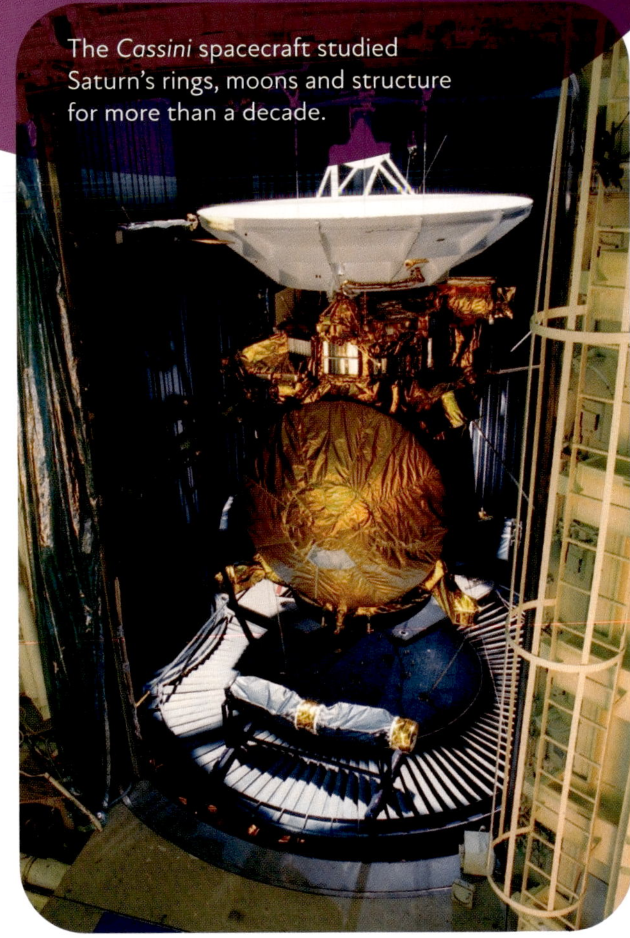

The *Cassini* spacecraft studied Saturn's rings, moons and structure for more than a decade.

The sixth planet

You can see Saturn in the night sky at certain times of the year. It's the furthest planet visible without a telescope. The planet is 1.2 billion kilometres away from Earth, even when the two planets are at their closest distance. Five missions have been sent to explore Saturn. *Cassini* was there between 2004 and 2017, exploring the moons and rings of the planet. Three space agencies and 17 nations contributed to the mission and much was learnt about the rings and the planet's internal structure. Saturn has at least 145 known moons; *Cassini* studied two of them (Titan and Enceladus) and found evidence of hydrothermal activity on Enceladus that potentially provides an environment suitable for microbes to live. One year on Saturn lasts for the equivalent of 10,759 days on Earth.

Put a ring on it

Saturn's rings are its most distinctive feature and are made from billions of small chunks of rock, ice and dust. The rings were formed by four key stages of evolution.

1. A comet or asteroid collided with one of Saturn's icy moons.
2. The impact resulted in billions of icy pieces that could not form another moon.
3. The icy debris spread around the planet, with more collisions continuing to occur.
4. The gravity of other moons shaped the rings.

FACT

It takes Saturn approximately 29 Earth years to complete one orbit around the Sun, and each of its seasons lasts more than seven years.

DID YOU KNOW?

Like Jupiter, Saturn is made mostly of hydrogen gas. It's less dense than water, which means it would float like an ice cube.

Quick five

1. The creamy colours of Saturn are generated by its atmosphere, superfast winds, and rising heat all combining to cause colour bands.
2. Saturn's volume is more than 760 Earths!
3. At NASA, they sometimes call Saturn the 'Real Lord of the Rings'.
4. The *Cassini* spacecraft orbited Saturn 294 times over the course of more than a decade.
5. Scientists believe that some of Saturn's moons might be able to support life.

FACT

Jupiter has several white, oval-shaped rotating storms in its southern hemisphere, as well as a huge swirling storm called the Great Red Spot.

Jupiter

Jupiter is 779 million kilometres from the Sun and takes 11.9 Earth years to orbit it. There's no land on Jupiter – it's made of liquid hydrogen. It is the largest of the planets. In fact, every other planet in the solar system could fit inside Jupiter! It spins extremely fast, turning once every 10 Earth hours.

What's in a name?
Jupiter is named for the king of all Roman gods.

Cloud belts
All we can see of Jupiter are the tops of cloud bands that circle the planet.

Bright clouds
The white areas are high, cold clouds made of ammonia crystals.

The Great Red Spot
This is a gigantic storm on Jupiter that has been raging for hundreds of years. It's so large that Earth could fit inside of it at least three times!

The Southern Aurora of Jupiter glows bright red because of hydrogen emissions.

Moons
Jupiter has more than 75 moons. These include four planet-sized moons and many smaller ones. Jupiter has the largest moon in our solar system – Ganymede is even larger than Mercury. Europa is thought to have abundant liquid water under its icy surface, and scientists think it might be one of the best places in the solar system to look for signs of life.

JUPITER

DID YOU KNOW?

Sizewise, if our Earth was a grape, Jupiter would be a basketball.

Look closer...
Jupiter has rings around it! Made of dust, they're very hard to see. Even though humans have known about Jupiter for thousands of years, the rings were only discovered in 1979 when the spacecraft *Voyager 1* visited Jupiter for the first time.

Busy planet
Nine spacecraft have visited Jupiter. Seven flew by and two orbited the gas giant. *Juno*, arrived at Jupiter in 2016, with NASA's *Europa Clipper* mission taking place in 2024.

JUNO

Mars

Mars is covered in a layer of iron-rich, red dusty soil. It has lots in common with the Earth. Its days are nearly the same length, although Martian years are almost double! Mars is 228 million kilometres from the Sun and takes 687 Earth days to orbit it.

Could humans live here?

The surface temperature on Mars ranges from -125 °C to 20 °C. It has an atmosphere, seasons, polar ice caps, and frozen water. Mars has two moons – Phobos and Deimos. They were probably once asteroids before they were pulled into Mars' orbit. The tallest mountain in the Solar System is found on Mars – Olympus Mons is three times taller than Mt Everest, and it is bigger than the state of Victoria!

Ice caps

An aerial view of the northern polar ice caps on Mars shows valleys as spiral bands.

Ice fog

Clouds and fog appear above the frozen cap on the southern polar region of Mars during springtime.

Water

Signs of water and ice have been detected on Mars.

DID YOU KNOW?

Australia's First Nations peoples used astronomy not only to navigate the land but also to create a natural calendar to track the availability of seasonal food.

Search for life

NASA's rover *Perseverance* is collecting rock samples and soil to help determine whether one day humans could live on Mars. Its official job is to search for any signs of life!

Dust devil

Whirling clouds of dust get picked up by warming air and then scattered across the Mars landscape.

Windy world

We cannot breathe the air on Mars because it is made up of 96% carbon dioxide. Scientists believe most of the atmosphere has been lost due to intense solar winds, which can hit speeds of up to 1,600,000 million kilometres an hour!

Alyssa Carson

Alyssa fell in love with the idea of becoming an astronaut when she was just three years old and wants to be one of the first astronauts to land on Mars. At 16, she was the youngest ever graduate of the Advanced Space Academy and the first person to ever finish all of NASA's space camps. She received her official certification to become an astronaut trainee.

'Technically, I'm allowed to fly into space, and just being able to say that, especially in my teens, feels amazing,' Alyssa said. NASA plans to launch a manned mission to Mars in 2030.

Jezero Crater

This crater is 45 km wide and is just north of the Martian equator. There is also evidence that a delta from a river once ran through it a very long time ago. It also contains clays, which only exist when water is present.

What's in a name?

Mars is named for the Roman god of war.

Earth

The Earth is the ideal planet for us. We orbit a sun that is the perfect size. If our Sun were much larger, the radiation from it would be too strong, but if it were much smaller, it wouldn't be strong enough to sustain life. Without the light and heat of the Sun, life wouldn't have survived. The atmosphere around our planet protects us, keeping temperatures at an appropriate level to sustain human life. The other important feature of our planet is the water that covers much of the surface. Without this liquid and the water-cycle sustained by our atmosphere, life on Earth wouldn't survive.

Quick five

1. Earth is not perfectly round – our planet has bulges.
2. Our gravity isn't uniform across the planet.
3. Our melting glaciers are making Earth wider.
4. About 4.6 billion years ago, our days were only six hours long!
5. The Earth is about 90,000 million kilometres away from the Sun.

FACT

Earth is the only planet known to support complex life.

The Sun and the seasons

Seasons occur because Earth is tilted as it orbits the Sun. When the northern part of the planet tilts towards the Sun, the Northern Hemisphere experiences summer and the Southern Hemisphere experiences winter. The opposite happens when the southern part of the planet tilts towards the Sun.

1. Northern spring
2. Southern autumn
3. Southern summer
4. Northern winter
5. Northern autumn
6. Southern spring
7. Southern winter
8. Northern summer

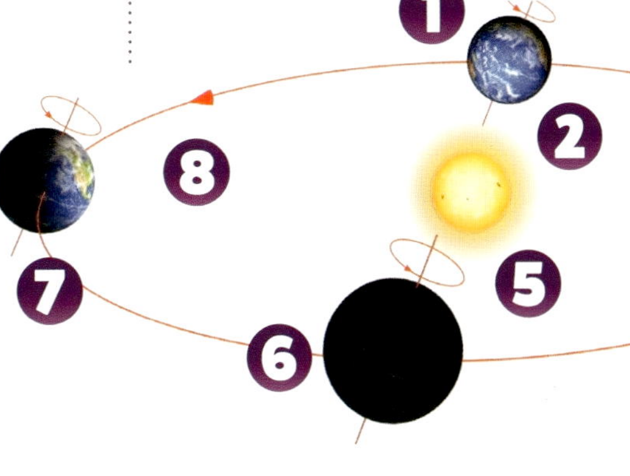

To the Moon

The Moon orbits the Earth once every 27 days – and it takes the same amount of time to rotate once on its axis. It is 384,400 km from Earth and controls the flow of the ocean's tides.

How continents were formed

Earth's continents, or landmasses, developed very slowly over time.

200 million years ago

Supercontinent Pangaea began breaking into two landmasses: Gondwana and Laurasia.

90 million years ago

The landmasses continued to break up and drift apart.

Today

The continents have spread across the globe.

The future

The Atlantic Ocean will widen, and the Mediterranean Sea will start to disappear.

DID YOU KNOW?

Elon Musk created his Space X aerospace company to help everyday earthlings travel to space.

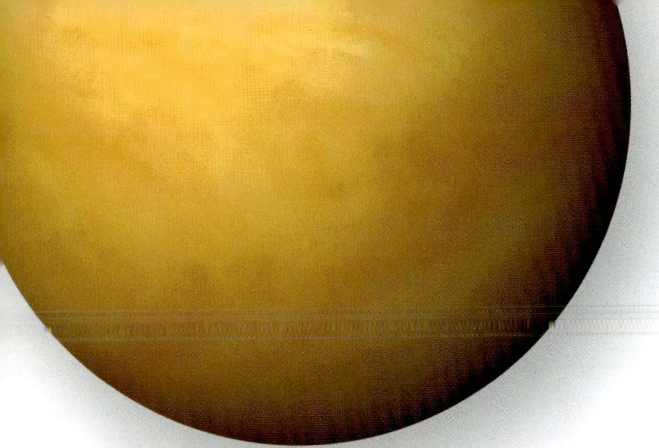

Venus

The second planet from the Sun is about the same size as Earth, but it's not a place you'd want to visit. It's the hottest planet in the solar system, with an average temperature of 462 °C. The atmosphere of Venus is more than 96% carbon dioxide, and it rains sulphuric acid. There are also many volcanoes on Venus, and scientists recently discovered 37 new ones that may be active.

Life on Venus

Earth's neighbouring planet is a volatile world of extreme heat and volcanic activity.

The greenhouse planet

The atmosphere on Venus actually traps heat in a runaway greenhouse effect, making it hotter than Mercury, even though Mercury is closer to the Sun. Truth is always stranger than fiction!

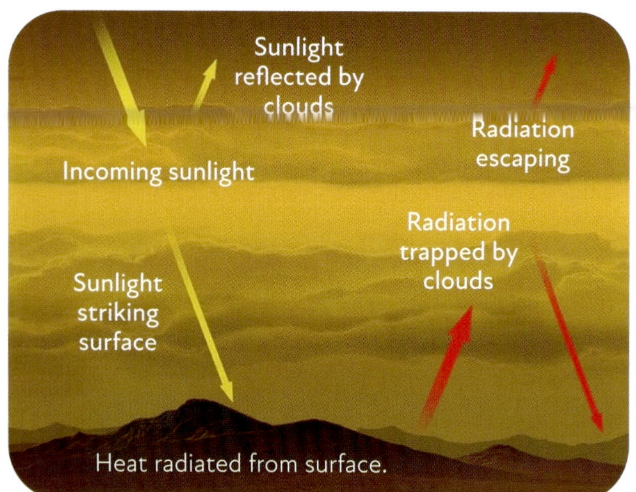

What's in a name?

Ancient Roman astronomers named Venus after their goddess of love and beauty.

Young and old

Venus looks quite young, as its surface doesn't have many craters, but its actual age is estimated to be about 4.6 billion years.

Could there be life?

The clouds on Venus contain phosphine, an indicator of possible microbial life.

Every day

One year on Venus lasts the equivalent of 243 Earth days.

Under pressure

The air pressure on Venus is 90 times more powerful than what we experience on the Earth's surface. In fact, it's as crushing as the pressure you'd feel at 2 km beneath the ocean here on Earth.

No moon

Venus does not have a moon – and scientists are yet to discover why. Mercury is the only other moonless planet, because it is so close to the Sun.

In a spin

Venus rotates in the opposite direction to the Earth, so the Sun always rises in the west and sets in the east.

Australia's First Nations peoples of the Great Victoria Desert noted how Jupiter and Venus always followed each other.

Look up!

The thick clouds that surround Venus reflect light, making it the brightest planet in our night sky. At various times throughout the year, you're able to spot Venus in the sky even without a telescope! Sometimes, the orbit of Earth and Venus line up in such a way that a 'Transit of Venus' occurs – when Venus passes in front of the Sun. The transits occur in pairs eight years apart, in a pattern that repeats every 243 years. Captain Cook studied the 1769 transit in Tahiti before going on to land for the first time at Botany Bay.

Visiting Venus

NASA first explored Venus in December 1962, when the spacecraft *Mariner 2* did a fly-by of the planet. In the decades since then, there have been several more missions, including a couple of landings that were cut short when Venus's harsh conditions destroyed the equipment. In June 2021, NASA announced three new missions with launches expected to take place between 2028 and 2030.

VENUS

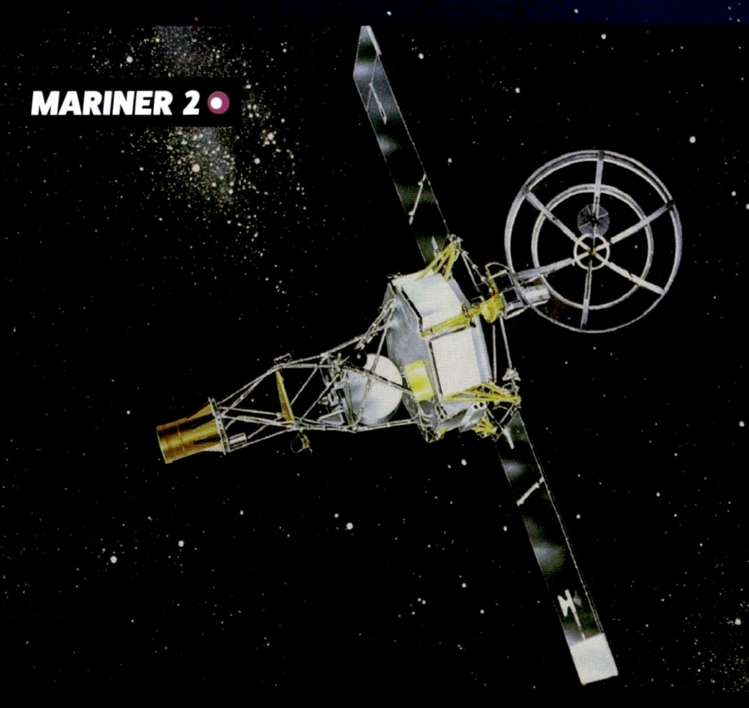
MARINER 2

Mercury

The smallest planet in our solar system and the closest to the Sun, Mercury looks like our Moon – grey and covered in craters. These craters are caused by the comets and asteroids that have hit the planet, most of them probably making their marks billions of years ago. It takes 88 Earth days for Mercury to orbit the Sun. No other planet has such extremes of heat and cold, with temperatures ranging from -180 °C to 430 °C.

What's in a name?

Mercury is named for the Roman messenger of the gods. It also shares its moniker with a metallic element that is liquid.

Small but mighty

With a diameter of 4878 km, Mercury is only a little bit larger than Earth's Moon. In the 1970s, scientists also discovered that the planet is shrinking, as its interior is slowly cooling.

Flying by

Two NASA spacecraft have visited Mercury. The first was *Mariner 10*, which visited in 1974–75 and flew by three times, taking pictures and collecting data. The second was *MESSENGER* (Mercury Surface, Space Environment, Geochemistry and Ranging), which orbited the planet between March 2011 and April 2015. In 2018, the European Space Agency launched *BepiColombo* to explore Mercury. It's expected to arrive at the planet on 5 December 2025.

Thin crust, thick core

Mercury is a very dense planet because of its large iron and nickel core. A huge impact billions of years ago probably removed some of the outer shell, leaving the planet with a thick core and thin crust.

1. An asteroid smashes into Mercury.
2. Direction of the shockwaves
3. Shockwaves
4. Crust
5. Mantle
6. Core
7. Shockwaves crack into crust.
8. Chaotic, messy terrain forms opposite the impact.

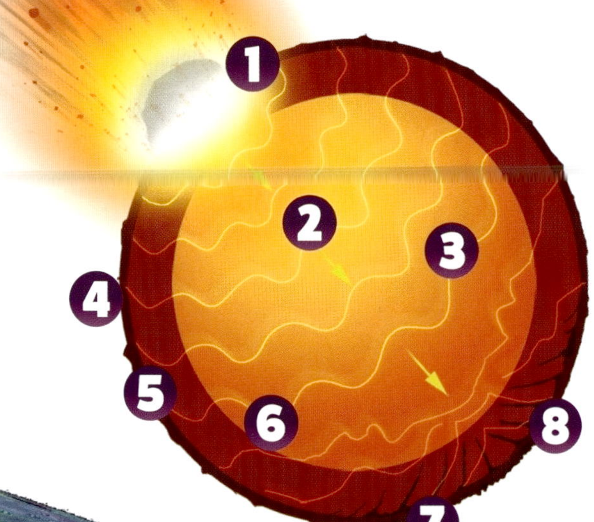

Special imaging techniques reveal Mercury's different types of terrain.

DID YOU KNOW?

The closer a planet is to the Sun, the faster it travels. Mercury travels at 47 km per second.

Surface level

Mercury's surface is marked by cliffs, highlands and craters, with some mountain ranges stretching hundreds of kilometres. The planet's largest crater, the Caloris Basin, is 1525 km wide – almost double the distance between Sydney and Melbourne – and is surrounded by mountains. It was caused by a meteor impact 3.8 billion years ago.

The air up there

Humans can't breathe on Mercury because the planet's atmosphere is made up of mostly oxygen, sodium, hydrogen, helium and potassium.

Highlands

These are usually older and more heavily cratered than the low plains.

Cliffs

Mercury has cliffs that formed when the planet cooled and cracked.

Craters

These last for billions of years because there is no air or water to erode them.

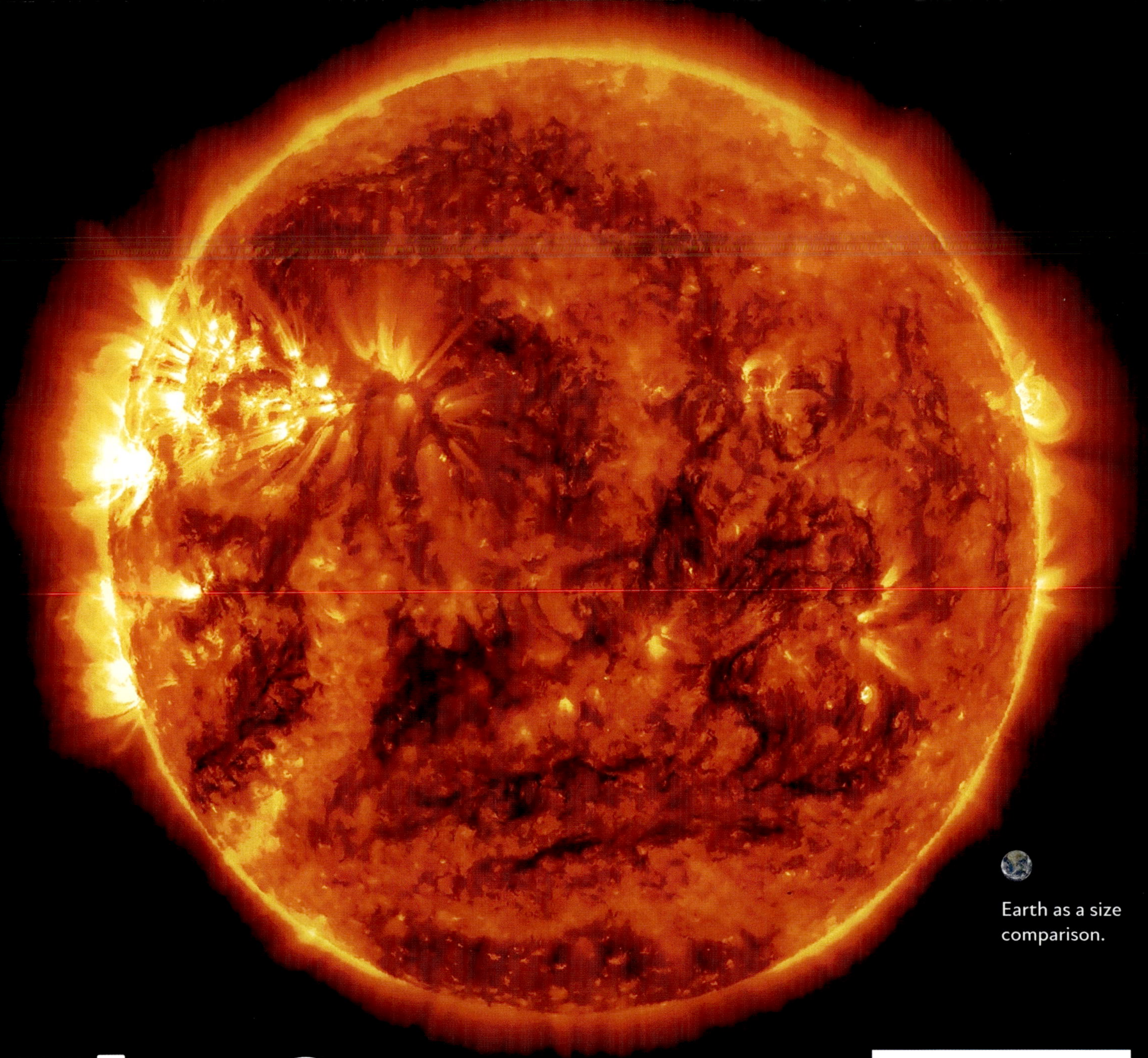

Earth as a size comparison.

The Sun

The Sun is the biggest object in our solar system. It has a diameter of 1,392,000 km and makes up 99.8% of our system's mass. It exerts an enormous gravitational force and dominates the motion of every celestial object in the solar system – including us! It is made up of hydrogen and helium and is held together by its own gravity.

Heliophysics

At NASA, a special division studies how the Sun and its constant release of particles, solar winds and magnetic system affects everything around it. This work is helping humanity better understand how the Sun has brought life to our system and, in turn, how that could happen elsewhere in the universe.

DID YOU KNOW?

The Sun is actually a yellow dwarf star!

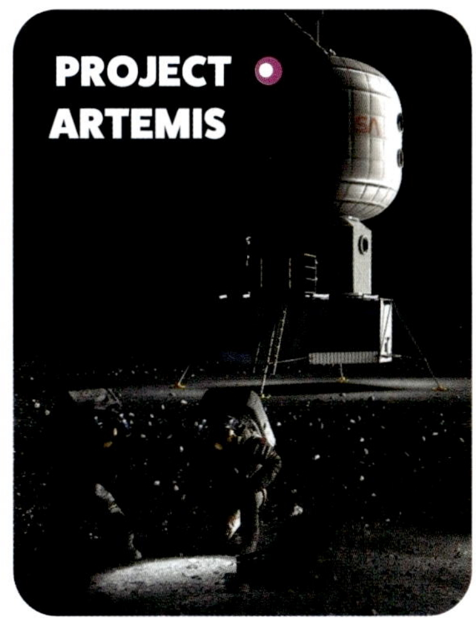

NASA woman

NASA is preparing to send the world's first woman of colour to the Moon as part of project Artemis. One of the main tasks for the team will be to study radiation in space to help collect data for humans to go deeper into space. The goal is to land a crew and have a permanent base for onwards exploration by the late 2020s.

Solar eclipse

When the Moon comes between Earth and the Sun, a solar eclipse occurs. Depending where you are on Earth when it happens, you can see the Sun partly or completely covered.

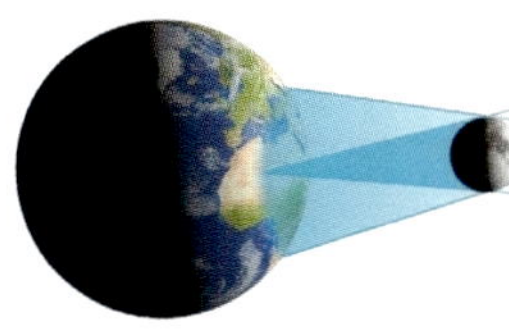

The Moon passes between the Earth and the Sun, casting a shadow on Earth.

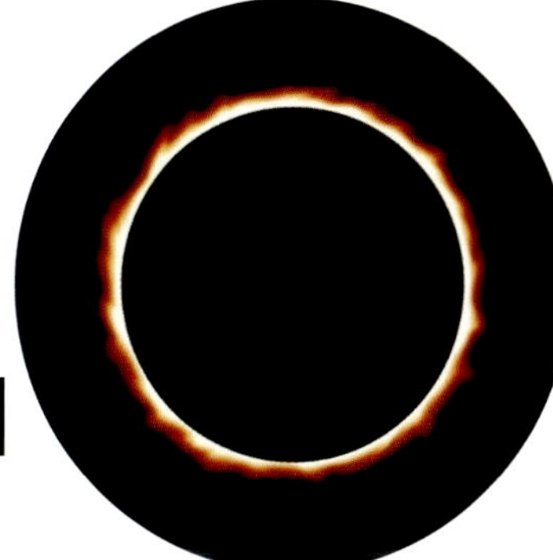

A total eclipse is when the bright disc of the Sun is completely covered.

Feeling small

Sunspots are areas of the Sun that are cooler than the rest of it. They aren't permanent, but they only occur when gas is trapped by a magnetic field. Although they appear to the naked eye to be small, a single sunspot is larger than Earth.

Bubble trouble

Huge bubbles of gas are occasionally ejected from the Sun and shoot across the solar system.

Space weather

The Sun is so powerful that its constant outpouring of energy can affect satellites, radio, GPS, spacecrafts and even power grids here on Earth. In 1989, a powerful solar-driven magnetic storm took out power in Quebec, causing 6 million people to lose electricity.

That's hot!

The surface temperature is about 5550 °C, but its core is 15,000,000 °C.

SUN

Inside a sunspot

1. A penumbra of brighter, hotter gas surrounds the umbra in larger spots.
2. The umbra is the dark, cooler core of the sunspot.
3. Sunspots extend deep into the top layer of the Sun.

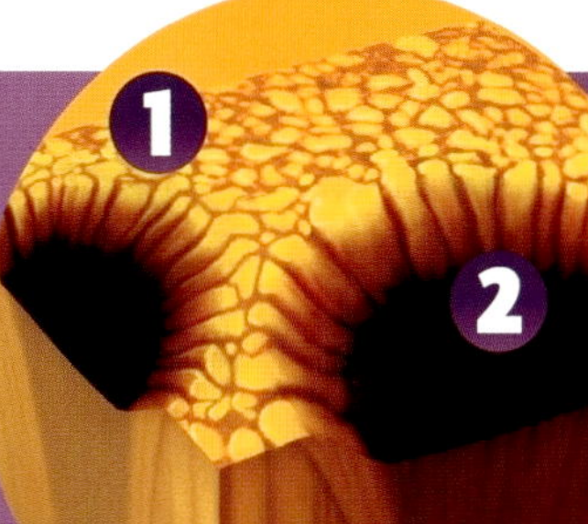

Moon gazing case study:

Redfern Jarjum School

It takes 27 days for the Moon to circle the Earth, and as it moves, we see it change from a thin sliver of light to a glowing ball. But as the Jarjum students discovered, the Moon doesn't glow from within – it just reflects the Sun!

FACT

Warrumbungle National Park in NSW was Australia's first Dark Sky Park. It's one of the best places in the world to see the Moon and stars.

On a cloudless night, there is so much to see if you take the time to look up. The further you are from big cities, the more stars come into view. The Redfern Jarjum College students all live close to Australia's biggest city, Sydney, so they can't always make out the stars very well – but they can still get a good look at the Moon when the sky is clear.

The Moon, Sun and sea

The Moon's gravity tugs at the Earth, creating bulges and dips in the ocean known as the 'tides'. The tides are also affected by the Earth's rotation and the Sun's gravitational pull.

You might have noticed that the Moon appears in different parts of the sky at different times, and it looks slightly different night after night. Sometimes you can even see it in the daytime! The Jarjum students had a good chat about night and day, the Sun, what they have seen of the Moon and what they know about it.

The Moon looks like it glows, but it is actually reflecting light from the Sun – the source of light in our solar system. When you look at the Moon, it looks like it is changing shape, but it is always an orb – a giant rock ball.

The students investigated how the appearance of the Moon changed from one night to the next. They used the darkest spot they could find at school, so they could make it like night-time. Their Moon was a softball, and they used a torch as the Sun.

DJ

SHAKIRA

The experiment

1. When the torch was in front of them, the ball seemed to be in shadow – like the new Moon.
2. When the torch was slightly to the side, only a narrow section of the ball appeared – like the crescent Moon.
3. When the light was halfway between, the ball appeared half in shadow – like a half-Moon.

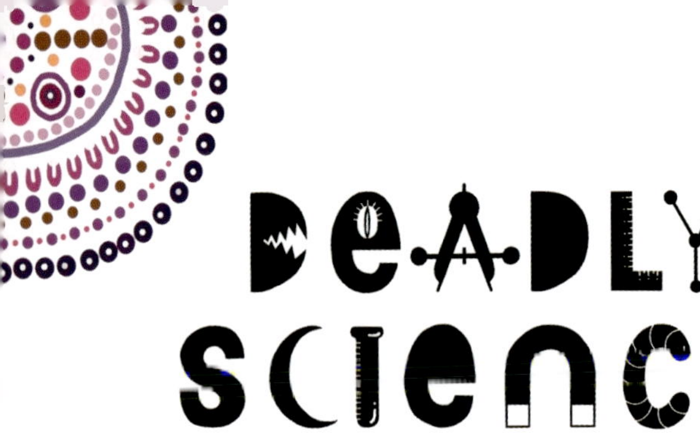

Deadly Science

The solar system

Hardie Grant acknowledges the Traditional Owners of the Country on which we work, the Wurundjeri People of the Kulin Nation and the Gadigal People of the Eora Nation, and recognises their continuing connection to the land, waters and culture. We pay our respects to their Elders past and present.

Hardie Grant Children's Publishing
Wurundjeri Country
Level 11, 36 Wellington Street
Collingwood Victoria 3066
Melbourne | Sydney | San Francisco
hardiegrant.com/childrens
www.australiangeographic.com.au
ISBN: 9781761216657
First published 2022
This edition published 2025

Series editor Corey Tutt **Illustrator** Mim Cole / Mimmim
Designer Harmony Southern

Publisher Penelope White **Editor** Savannah Hollis with Olivia Brown
Cover design Andy Warren **Internal design** Hannah Janzen
Production Sally Davis

Printed in China by LEO Paper Products LTD

The paper this book is printed on is from FSC® certified forests and other controlled sources. FSC® promotes environmentally responsible, socially beneficial and economically viable management of the world's forests.

10 9 8 7 6 5 4 3 2 1

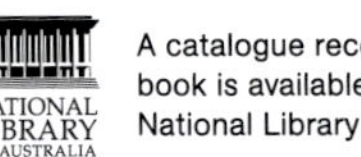

A catalogue record for this book is available from the National Library of Australia

Picture credits

Front Cover: freestyle images/Shutterstock (SS); 19 STUDIO/SS; Phonlamai Photo/SS; podestaphotos/SS; NASA images/SS; 3Dsculptor/SS. **1.** Corey Tutt/DS. **2:** Sergey Givens/SS; AlexLMX/SS; NASA/MSFC; SS. **3:** James Robbins/Dreamstime; NASA/JPL 2019. **4:** St Amir/SS. **5:** Alex Bascuas/SS, Australian Geographic (AG). **6–7:** NASA/JPL-Calteach. **7:** Terry Dell/SS; Catmando/SS; Paul Curnow/Australian Indigenous Astronomy. **8:** NASA images/SS; Jazziel/SS; BlueRingMedia/SS; Martin Capek/SS. **9:** Luke Tscharke/AG. **10:** NASA. **11:** NASA; J. Weston & Sons, Eastbourne/Wikipedia; AG.**12:** AG; AG; NASA/JPL-Caltech/Lunar & Planetary Institute; Borisb17/SS. **13:** Simon Wendler/SS; **14:** Gerhald/SS. **15:** Nicku/SS; NASA/JPL/STScl; Diego Barucco/SS. **16:** All NASA. **17:** NASA/JPL-Caltech/Space Science Institute. **18:** Vadim Sadoski/SS; **19:** Bill Dunford/NASA; Lightspring/SS; NASA/JPL-Caltech; NASA/JPL-Caltech/SwRI/ASI/INAF/JIRAM. **20–21:** esfera/SS. **21:** NASA/JPL-Caltech/MSSS/JHU-APL; National Air and Space Museum; Triff/SS. **22:** Harvepino/SS. **23:** NASA/NOAA; AG; AG; AG; Elena11/SS; 3Dsculptor/SS; violetkaipa/SS. **24:** All NASA. **25:** Anton27/SS; NASA-JPL-Caltech. **26:** NASA; NASA; NASA/Johns Hopkins University Applied Physics Laboratory/Carnegie Institution of Washington; ESA/ATG medialab; NASA. **27:** NASA. **28:** Triff/SS; **29:** All NASA. **30:** Elena11/SS; NASA. **31:** Deadly Science.